EXPLORING THE WORLD

CORONADO

Francisco Vásquez de Coronado
Explores the Southwest

BY ROBIN S. DOAK

Content Adviser: Professor Sherry L. Field, Department of Social Science Education,
College of Education, The University of Georgia

Reading Adviser: Dr. Linda D. Labbo, Department of Reading Education,
College of Education, The University of Georgia

COMPASS POINT BOOKS
MINNEAPOLIS, MINNESOTA

Compass Point Books
3722 West 50th Street, #115
Minneapolis, MN 55410

Visit Compass Point Books on the Internet at *www.compasspointbooks.com* or
e-mail your request to *custserv@compasspointbooks.com*

Editors: E. Russell Primm, Emily J. Dolbear, and Melissa McDaniel
Photo Researcher: Svetlana Zhurkina
Photo Selector: Catherine Neitge
Designer: Design Lab
Cartographer: XNR Productions, Inc.

Library of Congress Cataloging-in-Publication Data
Doak, Robin S. (Robin Santos), 1963–
Coronado: Francisco Vásquez de Coronado Explores the Southwest / by Robin S. Doak.
    p. cm. — (Exploring the world)
Includes bibliographical references and index.
ISBN 0-7565-0123-7
    1. Coronado, Francisco Vasquez de, 1510–1554—Juvenile literature. 2. Explorers—America—
Biography—Juvenile literature. 3. Explorers—Spain—Biography—Juvenile literature. 4. Southwest,
New—Discovery and exploration—Spanish—Juvenile literature. 5. America—Discovery and
exploration—Spanish—Juvenile literature. [1. Coronado, Francisco Vasquez de, 1510–1554.
2. Explorers. 3. Southwest, New—Discovery and exploration. 4. America—Discovery and exploration—Spanish.] I. Title. II. Series.
E125.V3 D65 2001
979'.01'092—dc21   2001001535

Table of Contents

An Amazing Journey Begins

On a cool winter day in 1540, a group of finely dressed Spanish **nobles** gathered in New Spain, which is now known as Mexico. The men had come to take part in a special journey. The leader of the group was Francisco Vásquez de Coronado. He hoped to find the rich cities of gold that were said to lie to the north.

Francisco Vásquez de Coronado and his group head north in search of new lands.

The group was one of the largest ever sent to explore the Americas. It was made up of more than 300 Spaniards and 1,000 native people. Huge herds of horses, mules, cattle, pigs, and sheep were also brought along. One of the travelers, Pedro de Castenada, later wrote about the trip. He called Coronado's group "the most brilliant company ever collected . . . to go in search of new lands."

Famed illustrator Frederic Remington drew a conquistador and his horses. The Spaniards' horses were the first ever seen by the Pueblo Indians.

At the head of the **expedition,** Coronado sat on his finest horse. His golden armor gleamed in the sunlight and the feather in his

A map of Coronado's journey

helmet swayed gently in the breeze. As the soldiers filed past him, each man placed his hand on a cross and a prayer book. They swore to follow God, the king of Spain, and Coronado himself. The men took the oath happily. They believed that gold and glory awaited them to the

Coronado's men swore their allegiance to Charles I, the king of Spain.

The first Europeans to explore the Great Plains

Coronado's conquistadors were the first Europeans to see the Grand Canyon.

north. They expected to return to New Spain as rich men, with amazing adventures to tell to their sons and daughters.

Coronado and his men would be gone for two years. They would travel more than 3,000 miles (4,827 kilometers) through the American Southwest. They would claim huge chunks of land for Spain. And they would be the first Europeans to live among the Pueblo Indians, explore the Great Plains, and see the Grand Canyon. Today, their trip is considered one of the most remarkable feats in exploration history. But in Coronado's lifetime, it was seen as a total failure.

A Mysterious World

Spain had controlled New Spain since 1521. That year, Hernán Cortés conquered the Aztec Indians, whose **empire** had stretched across the region. By the time of Coronado's expedition, other Spaniards had explored the lands south of New Spain. But no one had yet explored the vast area to the north.

Some people believed that great

Hernán Cortés conquered the Aztecs in 1521.

riches were to be found in the north. They had heard the legend of the Seven Cities of Cibola told by the native peoples of New Spain. According to the legend, the cities were filled with tall buildings with walls of gold. The walls were said to be studded with **turquoise** and other gems.

Antonio de Mendoza, the first **viceroy** of New Spain, had heard the legends, but he believed that the Seven Cities were the stuff of dreams. That changed in 1536, however, when a Spaniard named Álvar Núñez Cabeza de Vaca arrived in New Spain. Cabeza de Vaca was one of four men who had

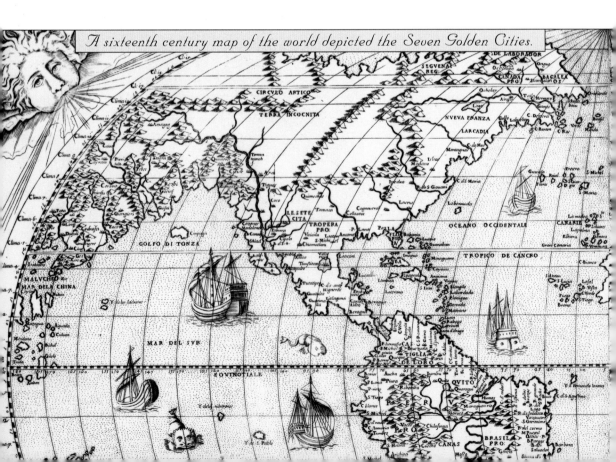

A sixteenth century map of the world depicted the Seven Golden Cities.

Álvar Núñez Cabeza de Vaca was one of four men to survive an expedition to Florida.

Cabeza de Vaca, who traveled from Florida to New Spain, heard tales of the Seven Cities of Cibola.

survived an expedition to Florida in 1527. For a number of years, Cabeza de Vaca had lived among the native peoples. The natives told him about large cities with tall buildings. They said these cities could be found to the north.

The viceroy began to wonder if these could be the Seven Cities of Cibola. In 1539, he decided that it was time to find out. The viceroy sent out a small party to scout the lands to the north. Five months later, the men returned with good news: The Seven Cities of Cibola were real! The leader of the group had seen one of these wonders with his own eyes.

*Cabeza de Vaca was the first European to mention
the buffalo, shown in this 1558 engraving.*

Choosing a Leader

Mendoza decided to send out a larger expedition to explore the golden cities. He chose Francisco Vásquez de Coronado, a nobleman and close friend, to lead the expedition.

Coronado was born in Salamanca, Spain, in 1510. From his earliest years, he seemed destined for fame.

Coronado as depicted in a mural by Gerald Cassidy in the Museum of New Mexico

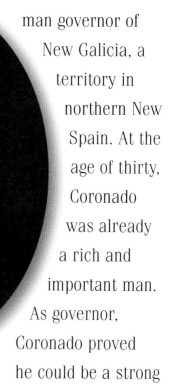

Antonio de Mendoza

A friend who predicted the young man's future told Coronado he would explore far-off lands. He said that Coronado would hold a high position with much power, but he added that the final part of Coronado's life would not be happy. He said Coronado would suffer a fall from which he would never recover.

Mendoza was named viceroy of New Spain in 1535. When he left Spain for New Spain, he took Coronado with him. A few years later, Mendoza made the young man governor of New Galicia, a territory in northern New Spain. At the age of thirty, Coronado was already a rich and important man. As governor, Coronado proved he could be a strong leader. He swiftly put down a slave uprising in his territory.

Coronado was also known for doing good deeds. So the viceroy believed that Coronado would treat the native people he met on the expedition with kindness, not cruelty.

To make sure the trip was a

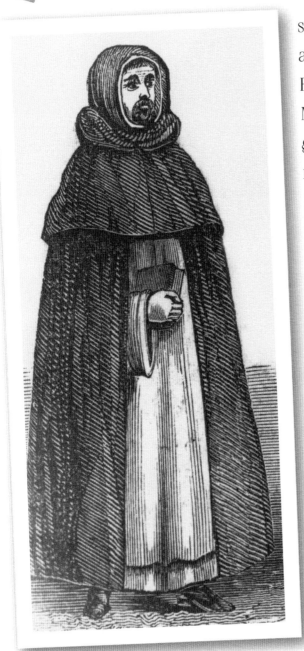

Marcos de Niza

success, Coronado brought along a Catholic priest named Fray Marcos de Niza. Fray Marcos and three other religious men would talk to the natives about God. But Fray Marcos joined the expedition for another important reason: He had led the earlier scouting trip to the north. Fray Marcos was the man who said he had seen one of the cities of Cibola. "The city from where I beheld it looked splendid," he had told the viceroy. "As well as I could judge, it is even larger than the city of Mexico." With Fray Marcos to lead them, Coronado believed that he would soon have the riches of Cibola in his hands.

The Journey of Death

As the men set off on February 23, 1540, they were in high spirits. But from the start, things went wrong. Fray Marcos had

Coronado and his men

*It is here, near Arizona's Montezuma Pass, that
Coronado entered the present United States.*

said that the roads were good and easy to travel over, but this was not true. The trails to the north were rough and dangerous. The group had to cross mountains and deserts. They even had to cross rivers filled with alligators.

Coronado sent a scout ahead to see how things looked. When the scout returned, he reported that he had seen very little silver or gold. Also, the natives he had talked to said that there were no grand cities nearby. Although Coronado tried to keep the scout's report a secret, the news got out to his men.

Coronado wrote home, describing the men's mood. He said, "The whole company felt disturbed at this, that a thing so much praised, and about which the father had said so many things, should be found [to be] so very different; and they began to think that all the rest would be of the same sort."

As spring stretched into summer, the weather and the rough journey began to take a toll. During the day, the group **sweltered** in the heat. At night, the men had to huddle together for warmth. The travelers suffered Indian attacks, snake bites, and sickness caused by eating poisonous plants. Some of the men died. As water and food began to run out, their spirits sank even lower. Some began calling the trip the "Journey of Death."

The Spanish fought with Indians during their journey.

The Death of a Dream

On July 7, 1540, Coronado and his men arrived at the first city of Cibola. The city, called Háwikuh, was a Zuni village with high stone walls. It was located in what is now western New Mexico. Háwikuh was the city that Fray Marcos claimed to have seen.

But Háwikuh did not look

New Mexico's Zuni pueblo, shown as it looked in the 1880s, was near Háwikuh, the first city of Cibola.

at all the way Fray Marcos had described it. He might have thought the city grand, but Pedro de Castenada did not. He called Háwikuh "a little crowded village . . . all crumpled together." Coronado's men were furious with the priest. "Such were the curses that some hurled at Fray Marcos that I pray God may protect him from them," wrote Castenada.

As Coronado and his

A Spanish conquistador

men approached Háwikuh, some of the villagers came outside. Coronado greeted them. He said he had come to claim the village in the name of the king of Spain and God. He told the villagers that he would do them no harm, as long as they **surrendered.** The people of the village were not impressed. They began to attack Coronado and his men. Although Coronado did not want to fight the Indians, he and his men needed to enter the village. They had traveled 1,500 miles (2,414 km), and their supplies had run out. Some of the men were dying of hunger. They needed food, so the starving Spaniards attacked the village.

Coronado, with his golden armor, was a prime target for the stones and arrows of the villagers. During the battle, Coronado was twice knocked from his horse by large stones. "If I had not been protected by the very good headpiece which I wore, I think that the outcome would have been bad for me," he later told the viceroy. After the second fall, Coronado was pulled

The battle of Háwikuh

Háwikuh had food but no riches.

to safety by two of his men.

The Spaniards were tired and hungry, but they managed to capture Háwikuh in just one hour. Inside the village, Coronado and his men found plenty of corn, beans, and turkey. What they did not find were riches. To the Zuni people, Háwikuh was an important village, a center of trade for all the nearby towns. But the residents of Háwikuh traded in animal hides, shells, and turkey feathers—not gold, silver, and gems. The Seven Cities of Cibola had turned out to be a tall tale.

Fray Marcos, fearing for his safety, headed back to New Spain. Coronado sent a letter to follow him. "I can assure you that in reality [Fray Marcos] has not told the truth in a single thing he said," he wrote to the viceroy. "The Seven Cities are seven little villages." Coronado told his friend that the only treasure he had found were some stone crystals and pieces of **emerald.**

Coronado found pueblo villages, not treasure.

A Glimmer of Hope

Coronado was disappointed, but he wanted to make the most of his trip. In his letter to the viceroy, he wrote, "I have determined to send [my men] throughout all the surrounding regions, in order to find out whether there is anything worthwhile."

Coronado's men explored the countryside that surrounded Háwikuh.

A conquistador

The Grand Canyon

Coronado sent out four small scouting parties to survey the area. One group was told to search the nearby villages of the Hopi people for riches. A second group was sent west to meet up with Spanish supply ships sent from New Spain. Neither group was successful.

A third group, led by García López de Cárdenas, was told to find the "great river" Coronado had heard of to the west. Cárdenas and his party journeyed to the south rim of the Grand Canyon. They were the first Europeans to view this natural wonder. Although the men searched for a way to descend to the bottom, they could not find one.

Hernando de Alvarado led the fourth group. He and twenty men were sent to explore the land to the east. Throughout his journey, Alvarado was greeted warmly by the people he met.

One village he visited was Acoma. This Pueblo Indian village is known as the "sky city" because it sits on top of a huge rock rising hundreds of feet above the surrounding plain. During their explorations, Alvarado and his men became the first Europeans to describe

Acoma pueblo and the Enchanted Mesa

*The Spaniards were the first Europeans to describe
the huge herds of buffalo that lived in the West.*

the huge herds of buffalo that roamed the plains.

At a village called Cicuye, Alvarado met an Indian his men nicknamed "the Turk." The Turk had an exciting tale to tell: Not only had he heard of the Seven Cities, he knew exactly where they were. They could be found in his homeland, a place called Quivira.

The tales the Turk spun were **fanciful** and amazing. He said the chief of the kingdom had a boat with a large golden eagle on the front. Each afternoon, the chief napped under a tree with small gold bells hanging from it. The bells put him to sleep as they chimed in the air. Gold was so common in Quivira, said the Turk, that everyone ate from plates made of gold.

Hernando de Alvarado

When Coronado learned of the Turk's stories, he was thrilled. Perhaps the journey would be a success after all! Coronado decided to head east to Quivira when spring arrived.

On to Quivira

On April 23, 1541, Coronado, his men, and the Turk left their winter camp. They may have traveled along the Arkansas River, following what is now known as the Santa Fe Trail. The men traveled all summer long, passing through the Texas Panhandle, Oklahoma, and into the center of what is now

The Turk leads Coronado in search of Quivira.

*Coronado's force moved through Palo Duro Canyon
in present-day West Texas.*

The Wichita Indians lived in huts with straw roofs.

Kansas. The farther Coronado went, the more **discouraged** he became. He was convinced that the Turk was lying to him.

When the group reached Quivira, they found just another Indian village. Quivira was the home of the Wichita people. Their homes were huts with straw roofs. Although Coronado found corn, pumpkins, and tobacco, again he found no riches.

The Turk had fooled them.

He admitted that he had been lying. He told Coronado that he had intended to lead Coronado and his men into the wilderness and then abandon them. He had hoped that, unable to find his way home, Coronado would die. The Spanish leader had the Turk executed.

Coronado Heights, west of Lindsborg, Kansas, is thought by some historians to be the spot where Coronado turned around and started back home.

Return to New Spain

Coronado's hopes were dashed. He and his men headed back to their winter camp. In a letter to the king of Spain, Coronado wrote of Quivira.

"And what I am sure of is that there is not any gold nor any other metal in all that country." Coronado also told the king that he did not feel that Spain

A fifteenth century mural from Kuaua pueblo in the present-day Coronado State Park. Coronado called the pueblo Tiguex.

Coronado's winter camp was at Kuaua pueblo, near present-day Bernalillo, New Mexico.

The Spanish used war dogs against the native people.

should found any settlements in the land to the north.

In early spring, Coronado fell off his horse and suffered severe injuries. When he recovered, he wanted only to

After his return, Coronado and his family lived in a palace in Mexico City.

go home. The group set out for New Spain. Two months later, Coronado and 100 of his men arrived home. The rest of the party straggled in later—weary, poor, and unhappy.

Most people in Spain and New Spain felt that Coronado's trip was a failure. Two years later, the explorer was brought to trial. He was accused of **mismanaging** the trip. It was also said that he had treated many native people cruelly. Coronado was not found guilty of any of the charges. One of his officers, however, was convicted of cruelty to native people.

On September 22, 1554, forty-four-year-old Coronado died in Mexico City. He never knew how important his trip really was. Several decades later, the Spanish would establish settlements in the land Coronado explored. These were some of the first European settlements in what would become the United States.

And much later, huge stores of silver, copper, and other valuable metals would be found in the American Southwest. The region did in fact hold great riches. They were there for the taking—just beneath the ground.

Father Juan de Padilla finds a cross erected by Coronado. The priest, who went to Kansas with the explorer, later returned there and was killed.

Glossary

discouraged having lost confidence

emerald a green jewel

empire a group of countries that have the same ruler

expedition a journey taken to find, learn, or acquire something; the group of people making the journey

fanciful showing imagination

mismanaging handling badly

nobles members of the ruling class

surrendered gave up

sweltered sweated

turquoise a blue gem

viceroy governor

Did You Know?

- Coronado was twenty-five years old when he traveled to New Spain.

- Coronado was married to Beatriz Estrada, the wealthy daughter of the colonial treasurer of New Spain.

- Coronado and his men thought that bison were some strange sort of cow.

- Shortly after Coronado returned from his expedition, he was relieved of his duties as governor and lived out the rest of his life as a minor government official in Mexico City.

Important Dates in Coronado's Life

1510
Coronado born in Salamanca, Spain

1536
Álvar Núñez Cabeza de Vaca arrives in New Spain telling tales of large cities with tall buildings

1540
Coronado and his expedition begin their search for the Seven Golden Cities

1554
Coronado dies in Mexico City

1542
Coronado returns to New Spain

1535
Antonio de Mendoza made Viceroy of New Spain

1539
Viceroy Mendoza sends a small party of explorers to scout the land to the north of New Spain

1521
Hernán Cortés conquers the Aztecs

Important People

HERNANDO DE ALVARADO (?) led a group of men from Coronado's expedition who became the first Europeans to see the High Plains region of the United States

ÁLVAR NÚÑEZ CABEZA DE VACA (C.1490–1560) Spanish explorer, member of 1527 expedition to Florida who lived among the Native Americans for several years before his return to New Spain in 1536

PEDRO DE CASTENADA (?) member of Coronado's group who later wrote an account of the expedition

FRANCISCO VÁSQUEZ DE CORONADO (1510–1554) Spanish explorer who led expedition in search of the Seven Cities of Cibola

HERNÁN CORTÉS (1485–1547) Spanish conqueror of Mexico

GARCÍA LÓPEZ DE CÁRDENAS (?) Spanish explorer, member of Coronado's expedition who led the group of first Europeans to see the Grand Canyon

ANTONIO DE MENDOZA (C.1490–1552) first viceroy of New Spain, put Coronado in charge of the expedition in search of the Seven Cities of Cibola

FRAY (FRIAR) MARCOS DE NIZA (C.1495–1558) missionary and explorer who claimed to have seen one of the Seven Cities of Cibola

"THE TURK" (?) Native American who told Coronado that the Seven Cities were in his homeland of Quivira

Want to Know More?

At the Library

Crisfield, Deborah and Patrick O'Brien, (illustrator). *The Travels of Francisco de Coronado*. Austin, Tex.: Raintree Steck-Vaughn, 2001.

Marcovitz, Hal. *Francisco Coronado and the Exploration of the American Southwest (Explorers of the New World)*. Broomall, Penn.: Chelsea House, 2000.

Weisberg, Barbara, Alex Haley, and Michael Eagle, (illustrator). *Coronado's Golden Quest*. Austin, Tex.: Raintree Steck-Vaughn, 1996.

On the Web

Francisco Vásquez de Coronado
http://www.win.tue.nl/~engels/discovery/coronado.html
For a brief biography of Coronado and links to many other
web sites with information on Coronado

Desert USA: Francisco Vásquez de Coronado,
A Most Famous Failing
http://www.desertusa.com/mag98/sep/papr/coronado.html
For a short biography and picture of Coronado

Kid Info—Explorers
http://www.kidinfo.com/American_History/Explorers.html
For links to information on Coronado and many other
explorers of the Americas

Through the Mail

Arizona Office of Tourism
2702 N. 3rd Street, Suite 4015
Phoenix, AZ 85004
888/520-3433
For information on travel to the state of Arizona

On the Road

Coronado National Memorial
4101 E. Montezuma Canyon Road
Hereford, AZ 85615
Visitor Information 520/366-5515
To visit the National Park Service memorial dedicated to
Coronado's exploration of the Southwestern United States

Index

About the Author

Robin S. Doak has been writing for children for more than fourteen years. A former editor of *Weekly Reader* and *U*S*Kids* magazine, Ms. Doak has authored fun and educational materials for kids of all ages. Some of her work includes: *FOSS Science Stories: Mixtures and Solutions, Human Body, Measurement,* and *Food and Nutrition; American Immigration; Dark Skies: Alien Invasion* and *The Awakening; The Associated Press Library of Disasters: Earthquakes & Tsunamis, Fires & Explosions, Volcanoes,* and *Wild Weather; Pro Sports Hall of Fame: Hockey.* Ms. Doak is a past winner of an Educational Press Association of America Distinguished Achievement Award. She lives with her husband and three children in central Connecticut.